HAL LEONARD

GUITAR METHOD
Supplement to Any Guitar Method

EASY POP CHRISTMAS MELODIES

T0082000

INTRODUCTION

Welcome to *Easy Pop Christmas Melodies*, a collection of 15 Christmas favorites arranged for easy guitar. If you're a beginning guitarist, you've come to the right place; these well-known songs will have you playing, reading, and enjoying music in no time!

This collection can be used on its own or as a supplement to the *Hal Leonard Guitar Method* or any other beginning guitar method. The songs are arranged in order of difficulty. Each melody is presented in an easy-to-read format—including lyrics to help you follow along and chords for optional accompaniment (by your teacher, if you have one).

USING THE AUDIO

Easy Pop Christmas Melodies is available as a book/audio package so you can practice playing with a real band. Each audio track begins with a full (or partial) measure of clicks, which sets the tempo and prepares you for playing along. To tune your guitar to the audio, use the track named "Tuning Notes."

Speed • Pitch • Balance • Loop

To access audio visit:
www.halleonard.com/mylibrary

Enter Code
6445-4685-4116-8364

ISBN 978-1-4584-0795-5

7777 W. BLUEMOUND RD. P.O. BOX 13819 MILWAUKEE, WI 53213

For all works contained herein:
Unauthorized copying, arranging, adapting, recording, Internet posting, public performance,
or other distribution of the printed or recorded music in this publication is an infringement of copyright.
Infringers are liable under the law.

Visit Hal Leonard Online at
www.halleonard.com

SONG STRUCTURE

The songs in this book have different sections, which may or may not include the following:

Intro
This is usually a short instrumental section that "introduces" the song at the beginning.

Verse
This is one of the main sections of a song and conveys most of the storyline. A song usually has several verses, all with the same music but each with different lyrics.

Chorus
This is often the most memorable section of a song. Unlike the verse, the chorus usually has the same lyrics every time it repeats.

Bridge
This section is a break from the rest of the song, often having a very different chord progression and feel.

Solo
This is an instrumental section, often played over the verse or chorus structure.

Outro
Similar to an intro, this section brings the song to an end.

ENDINGS & REPEATS

Many of the songs have some new symbols that you must understand before playing. Each of these represents a different type of ending.

1st and 2nd Endings
These are indicated by brackets and numbers. The first time through a song section, play the first ending and then repeat. The second time through, skip the first ending, and play through the second ending.

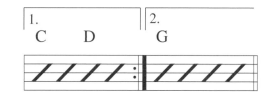

D.S.
This means "Dal Segno" or "from the sign." When you see this abbreviation above the staff, find the sign (𝄋) earlier in the song and resume playing from that point.

al Coda
This means "to the Coda," a concluding section in the song. If you see the words "D.S. al Coda," return to the sign (𝄋) earlier in the song and play until you see the words "To Coda," then skip to the Coda at the end of the song, indicated by the symbol: ⊕.

al Fine
This means "to the end." If you see the words "D.S. al Fine," return to the sign (𝄋) earlier in the song and play until you see the word "Fine."

D.C.
This means "Da Capo" or "from the head." When you see this abbreviation above the staff, return to the beginning (or "head") of the song and resume playing.

CONTENTS

GOOD KING WENCESLAS

Words by JOHN M. NEALE
Music from Piae Cantiones

Verse

Copyright © 2011 by HAL LEONARD CORPORATION
International Copyright Secured   All Rights Reserved

JOLLY OLD ST. NICHOLAS

Traditional 19th Century American Carol

Copyright © 2011 by HAL LEONARD CORPORATION
International Copyright Secured   All Rights Reserved

AWAY IN A MANGER

Words by JOHN T. McFARLAND
Music by JAMES R. MURRAY

Copyright © 2011 by HAL LEONARD CORPORATION
International Copyright Secured   All Rights Reserved

6

THE CHIPMUNK SONG

Words and Music by
ROSS BAGDASARIAN

Copyright © 1958 Bagdasarian Productions LLC
Copyright Renewed
International Copyright Secured   All Rights Reserved

CAROLING, CAROLING

Words by WIHLA HUTSON
Music by ALFRED BURT

TRO - © Copyright 1954 (Renewed) and 1957 (Renewed) Hollis Music, Inc., New York, NY
International Copyright Secured
All Rights Reserved Including Public Performance For Profit
Used by Permission

O COME, O COME IMMANUEL

Plainsong, 13th Century
Words translated by JOHN M. NEALE
and HENRY S. COFFIN

Copyright © 2011 by HAL LEONARD CORPORATION
International Copyright Secured   All Rights Reserved

GRANDMA GOT RUN OVER
BY A REINDEER

Words and Music by
RANDY BROOKS

Chorus

Grand-ma got run o-ver by a rein-deer walk-ing home from our house Christ-mas Eve. You can say there's no such thing as San-ta, but as for me and Grand-pa, we be-lieve.

Verse

1. She'd been drink-ing too much egg-nog
2., 3. *See additional lyrics*

and we begged her not to go. But she for-got her med-i-ca-tion, and she stag-gered out the door in-to the snow.

Copyright © 1979 Kris Publishing (SESAC) and Elmo Publishing (SESAC)
All Rights Controlled and Administered by BMG Chrysalis
All Rights Reserved   Used by Permission

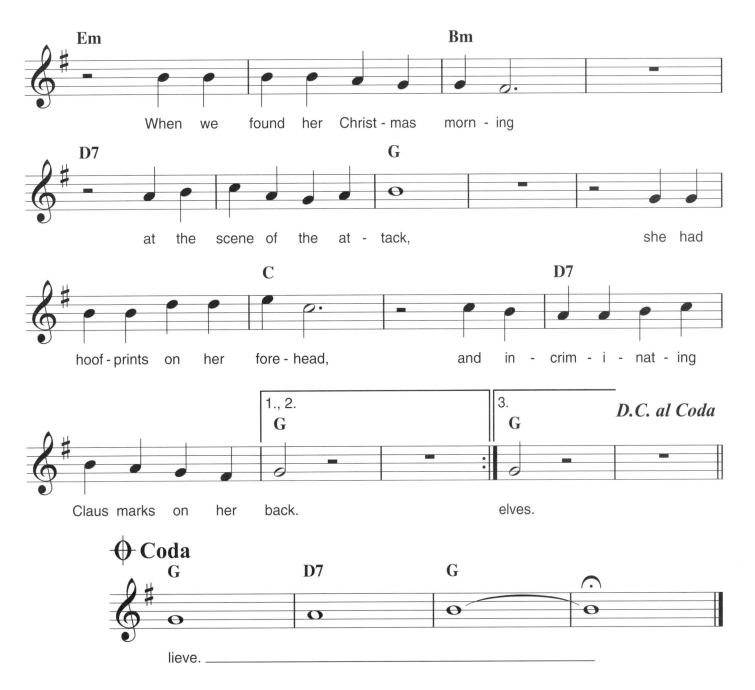

Additional Lyrics

2. Now we're all so proud of Grandpa,
   He's been taking this so well.
   See him in there watching football,
   Drinking beer and playing cards with Cousin Mel.
   It's not Christmas without Grandma.
   All the family's dressed in black,
   And we just can't help but wonder;
   Should we open up her gifts or send them back?

3. Now the goose is on the table,
   And the pudding made of fig.
   And the blue and silver candles,
   That would just have matched the hair in Grandma's wig.
   I've warned all my friends and neighbors,
   Better watch out for yourselves.
   They should never give a license
   To a man who drives a sleigh and plays with elves.

JINGLE BELLS

Words and Music by
J. PIERPONT

Copyright © 2011 by HAL LEONARD CORPORATION
International Copyright Secured   All Rights Reserved

Chorus

Jin - gle bells, jin - gle bells, jin - gle all the

way. Oh, what fun it is to ride in a

one horse o - pen sleigh! _____ Jin - gle bells,

jin - gle bells, jin - gle all the way.

Oh, what fun it is to ride in a

one horse o - pen sleigh!

A HOLLY JOLLY CHRISTMAS

Music and Lyrics by
JOHNNY MARKS

Verse

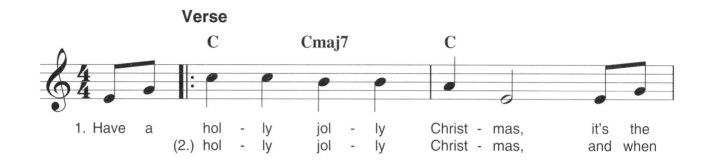

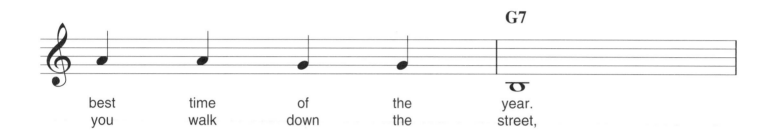

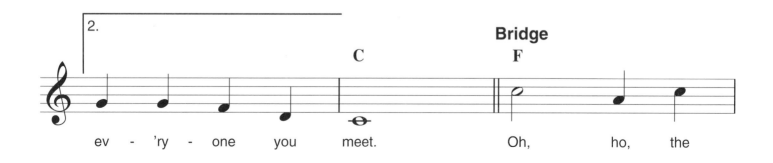

Copyright © 1962, 1964 (Renewed 1990, 1992) St. Nicholas Music Inc., 1619 Broadway, New York, New York 10019
All Rights Reserved

mis - tle - toe hung where you can see.

Some - bod - y waits for you, kiss her once for

Outro

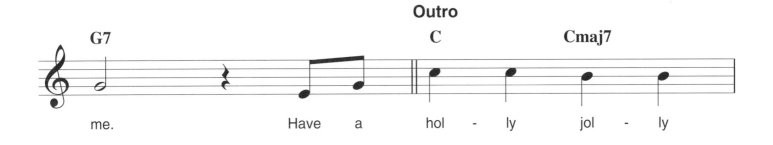

me. Have a hol - ly jol - ly

Christ - mas, and in case you did - n't hear,

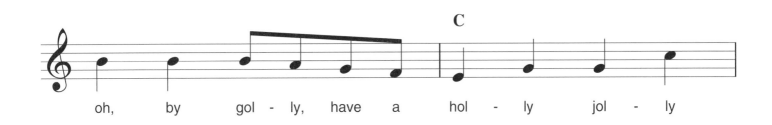

oh, by gol - ly, have a hol - ly jol - ly

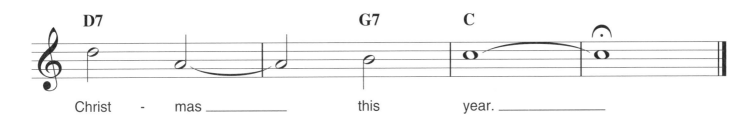

Christ - mas _____ this year. _____

DO YOU HEAR WHAT I HEAR

Words and Music by NOEL REGNEY
and GLORIA SHAYNE

Verse

1. Said the night-wind to the lit-tle lamb,
2., 3., 4. *See additional lyrics*

do you see what I see?

Way up in the sky, lit-tle lamb,

do you see what I see? A

star, a star, danc-ing in the night, with a

To Coda

tail as big as a kite, with a tail as big as a

Copyright © 1962 (Renewed) by Jewel Music Publishing Co., Inc. (ASCAP)
International Copyright Secured   All Rights Reserved
Used by Permission

kite.   2., 3. Said the   4. Said the

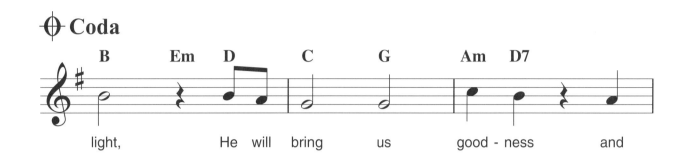

light,   He will bring us   good - ness   and

light. _____

Additional Lyrics

2. Said the little lamb to the shepherd boy,
 Do you hear what I hear?
 Ringing through the sky, shepherd boy,
 Do you hear what I hear?
 A song, a song, high above the tree,
 With a voice as big as the sea,
 With a voice as big as the sea.

3. Said the shepherd boy to the mighty king,
 Do you know what I know?
 In your palace warm, mighty king,
 Do you know what I know?
 A Child, a Child shivers in the cold,
 Let us bring Him silver and gold,
 Let us bring Him silver and gold.

4. Said the king to the people ev'rywhere,
 Listen to what I say!
 Pray for peace, people ev'rywhere,
 Listen to what I say!
 The Child, the Child, sleeping in the night;
 He will bring us goodness and light,
 He will bring us goodness and light.

YOU'RE ALL I WANT FOR CHRISTMAS

Words and Music by GLEN MOORE
and SEGER ELLIS

Intro

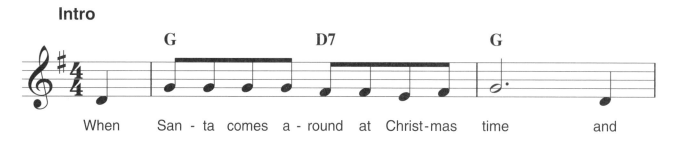

When San-ta comes a-round at Christ-mas time and

leaves a lot of cheer at ev-'ry door, if

he would on-ly grant the wish in my heart,

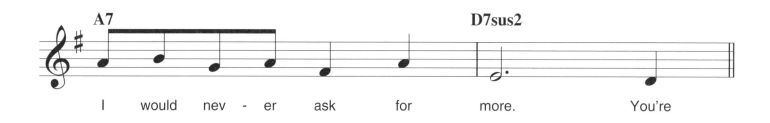

I would nev-er ask for more. You're

Chorus

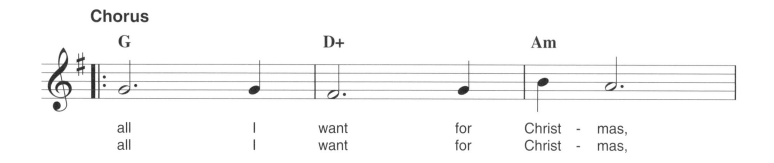

all I want for Christ - mas,
all I want for Christ - mas,

Copyright © 1948 SONGS OF UNIVERSAL, INC.
Copyright Renewed
All Rights Reserved   Used by Permission

all I want my whole life
and if all my dreams come

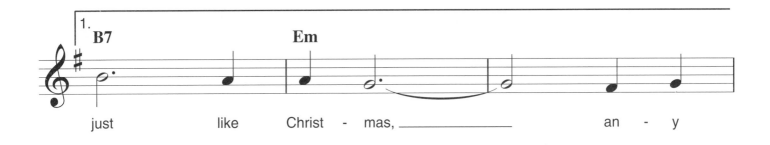

through. _____ Each day is
true, _____ then I'll a -

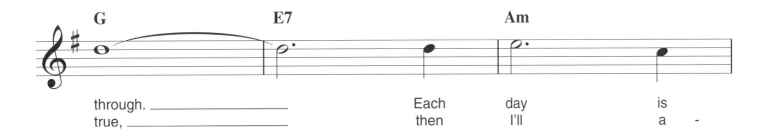

just like Christ - mas, _____ an - y

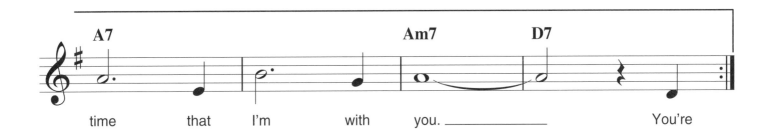

time that I'm with you. _____ You're

wake on Christ - mas morn - ing and find

my stock - ing filled with you. _____

LET IT SNOW! LET IT SNOW! LET IT SNOW!

Words by SAMMY CAHN
Music by JULE STYNE

Copyright © 1945 by Producers Music Publishing Co., Inc. and Cahn Music Co.
Copyright Renewed
All Rights for Producers Music Publishing Co., Inc. Administered by Chappell & Co.
All Rights for Cahn Music Co. Administered by WB Music Corp.
International Copyright Secured   All Rights Reserved

lights   are   turned   way   down   me   low, }
long   as   you   love   me   so, }   let   it

To Coda ⊕

snow,   let   it   snow,   let   it   snow!   When   we

Bridge

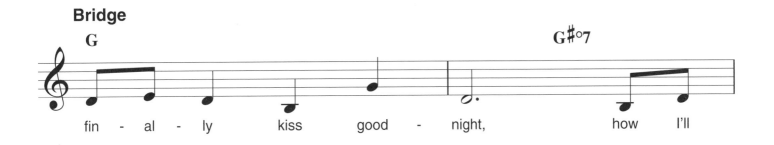

fin - al - ly   kiss   good - night,   how   I'll

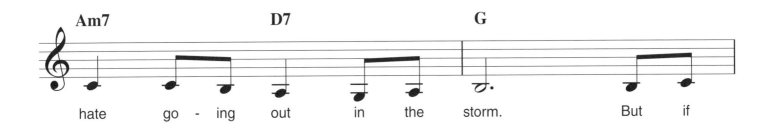

hate   go - ing   out   in   the   storm.   But   if

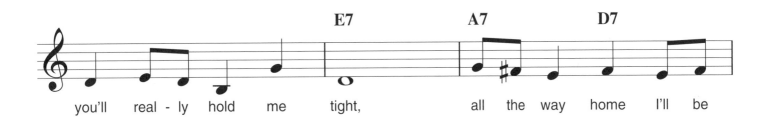

you'll   real - ly   hold   me   tight,   all   the   way   home   I'll   be

D.S. al Coda   ⊕ **Coda**

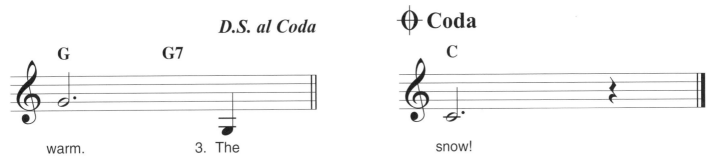

warm.   3. The   snow!

SILVER BELLS
from the Paramount Picture THE LEMON DROP KID

Words and Music by JAY LIVINGSTON
and RAY EVANS

Copyright © 1950 Sony/ATV Music Publishing LLC
Copyright Renewed
All Rights Administered by Sony/ATV Music Publishing LLC, 8 Music Square West, Nashville, TN 37203
International Copyright Secured   All Rights Reserved

HERE COMES SANTA CLAUS
(RIGHT DOWN SANTA CLAUS LANE)

Words and Music by GENE AUTRY
and OAKLEY HALDEMAN

© 1947 (Renewed) Gene Autry's Western Music Publishing Co.
All Rights Reserved   Used by Permission

SANTA CLAUS IS COMIN' TO TOWN

Words by HAVEN GILLESPIE
Music by J. FRED COOTS

© 1934 (Renewed 1962) EMI FEIST CATALOG INC.
Rights for the Extended Renewal Term in the United States Controlled by HAVEN GILLESPIE MUSIC and EMI FEIST CATALOG INC.
All Rights for HAVEN GILLESPIE MUSIC Administered by LARRY SPIER MUSIC, LLC
All Rights outside the United States Controlled by EMI FEIST CATALOG INC. (Publishing) and ALFRED PUBLISHING CO., INC. (Print)
All Rights Reserved   Used by Permission